The WOBBLY WALLABY
and the Absolute Bandicoot

Written by PREMA NISHAN

Illustrated by POLINA HRYTSKOVA

Cover Image: Polina Hrytskova
Cover Design: MoonCow Studios
Layout and Typesetting: Mooncow Studios
Illustrator: Polina Hyrtskova

PREMA
NISHAN STORIES
SECRETLY SACRED AND SILLY STORIES

www.premanishanstories.com

For all the
WILD
and
WONDERFUL
wobbly ones
of the
world...

The Wobbly Wallaby
wobbled unwillingly.

She tried to go straight,
but went instead WILLY-NILLY-LY!

All the other wallabies
in straight lines they would hop
but the Wobbly Wallaby
WOBBLED
all over the shop.

The Wobbly Wallaby
would never win any race
because she was always
hopping ALL OVER THE PLACE.

She would hop to one thing
and very quick to the next

always looking for the thing
that was BEST.

On her way to the meadow,
she might see a nice FLOWER

and then she might WANDER
to the lake for an hour,

and when she would finally
get back on her way,
she might find a
FAT WOMBAT
who wanted to play.

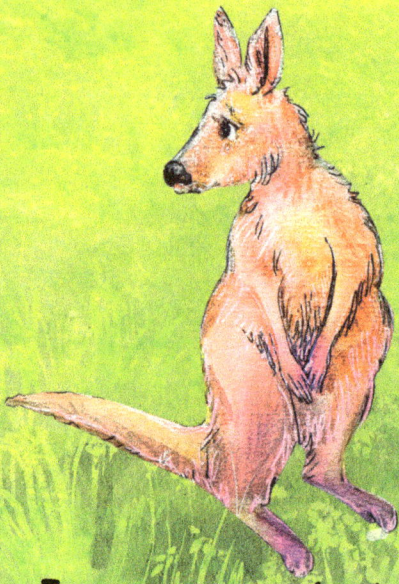

It appeared that the way which was right and correct

was to hop on a path that was straight and direct.

But if she tried to be still, her wobble only got **WILDER**

she just couldn't contain that **WOBBLE** inside her.

She would hop over here
and hop over there

the others had already gone,
and she tried not to care...

But why did this Wobbly Wallaby
wobble so wildly?

And why could she never
be still or sit idly?

What made her so WOBBLY
and RESTLESS inside?
She couldn't do one thing for long,
no matter how hard she tried.

Wobbly Wallaby sometimes felt a bit SAD.

Sometimes she wanted what those other wallabies had.

Those wallabies that were FOCUSED and could JUMP VERY STRAIGHT,

got the juiciest grasses because they never were late.

One day she sat near a big tree by the root
and spotted a cute little BANDICOOT.

She said, "Hi Mr Bandicoot,
would you like to play?"

He said, "No I don't,
so just go away.

Go play with someone
who jumps around like you
and leave me alone –
I've got important things to do."

Now Wobbly felt HURT
and her eyes filled with TEARS.

It was same thing that happened
through all of her years!

She tried to make friends
but when she reached out to play,

most creatures she met
seemed to TURN AWAY.

The Bandicoot said,
"Now you don't have to cry.
I'm just telling you straight,
because I DON'T LIKE TO LIE.

For the last three days
I've found nothing to eat
so I'm working to dig out
a nice LITTLE TREAT.

I am a creature who
stays all alone –
better you GO PLAY with
some friends of your own."

Wobbly could not hold back her **TEARS** any longer!

She cried and she wept and she wailed even stronger!

"Those other wallabies think I do everything **WRONG** because I can't focus on one thing at a time for long."

Now Bandicoot stopped
and for a minute he THOUGHT
about the difficult place
where the wallaby was caught.

He said, "Well now,
miniature kangaroo,
about your WOBBLY PROBLEM,
I don't know what to do.

But I'm a very
solitary creature,
so perhaps in this case
I can be a GOOD TEACHER."

"I'm very FOCUSED and
I DON'T LIKE DISTRACTIONS –
sometimes I struggle
to show care in my actions.

I dig holes BY MYSELF
and I find my own food.
I don't need any help,
and SOMETIMES I SEEM RUDE.

But I think I may discover
something from you,
even if you're
A WOBBLY KANGAROO.

She said, "Well I'm no kangaroo, but I do like to be with other creatures, even if they're different to me.

Perhaps if you had
some others around
they'd HELP YOU to dig
better holes in the ground.

I could dig holes,
just look at my PAWS!

Together would be better
than only with yours."

Wobbly bent down
and she started to dig.
In no time she'd
dug up a hole very big!

It wasn't too straight,
it was a WOBBLY HOLE...

But it was the
perfect alignment
to REACH to the GOAL!

Then suddenly Bandicoot
saw what she'd found –
a nice juicy,
WRIGGLY WORM
in the ground!

Bandicoot hungrily
jumped on that dinner

that's when he realised
he was onto a WINNER!

He said,
"I'm sorry Miss Wallaby, I do beg your pardon!
I was frantically digging one hole in the garden!

Too busy to see
that a FRIEND like you
can remind me to

LOOK

around me too.

Instead of just burying my head in the ground,
I can CONNECT with the other creatures around.

To reach to my goal I can COLLABORATE;
and holes that find worms
don't always need to be straight!"

"Thanks,
Mr Bandicoot!"
The wallaby said.

"I'd thought I should be more like the others instead.
But something that now I am beginning to know:

That life's not about where you get to,
but about HOW YOU GO!

I can be wobbly, but still I may find
treasures and pleasures of a wonderful kind.

I can love my adventures,
and FIND JOY in my play –
Even if it's a different
and a WOBBLY WAY."

THE END!

THE AFTER-WOBBBBLE

The Wobbly Wallaby is always jumping here and there. All the things she comes across grab her attention; she has difficulty staying still or focusing for long at all! She goes in one direction, and then gets distracted and changes track; she struggles to stick to her goals and she's always late! She just doesn't seem to be able to behave in the same way as the other wallabies. We're not giving her any diagnoses, but if the Wobbly Wallaby happened to be a kid in a classroom, some might even say she had ADHD.

The Absolute Bandicoot is at first annoyed by Wobbly Wallaby. He is the complete opposite – he can't see anything outside the one straight hole he is fixed on digging. He doesn't like disturbance, and wants to stay focused on his singular task. He tends to be a little rude and abrupt, which hurts the sensitive wallaby's feelings. But these two quite different and special creatures find that they have some gifts to share with each other, and they realise in the end that they help each other, and they make a great team!

The Wobbly Wallaby and the Absolute Bandicoot tells the tale of the wobbly ones. It hopes to normalise, to celebrate, bring awareness to the creative power of the wobble! To help us to recognise genius

emerging from those wobbles, to feel the liberation from the linear, the breaking free from the fixed and the typical. To also acknowledge that there are challenges that come with a distractable and differently-shaped mind, and to point to the unsaid expectations, shames and pressures that can live inside the wobbly ones.

I'm sure most of us can recognise parts of ourselves in these apparently neurodiverse marsupials! I know I certainly do! Kids learning to understand their gifts alongside their challenges becomes an essential part of harnessing their genius, understanding and accepting themselves and using their gifts to create their own unique magic – just as the wallaby and the bandicoot have done together.

The Wobbly Wallaby and the Absolute Bandicoot is the third book published by Prema Nishan. Look out for **Dichotomous Hippopotamus and the Half-and-half Giraffe**, as well as **The Irrelevant Elephant and the Horse of Remorse** – all are fun rhyming stories about our inner selves and finding harmony.

PREMA NISHAN STORIES
SECRETLY SACRED AND SILLY STORIES

Check out **www.premanishanstories.com** for more information and to order books!

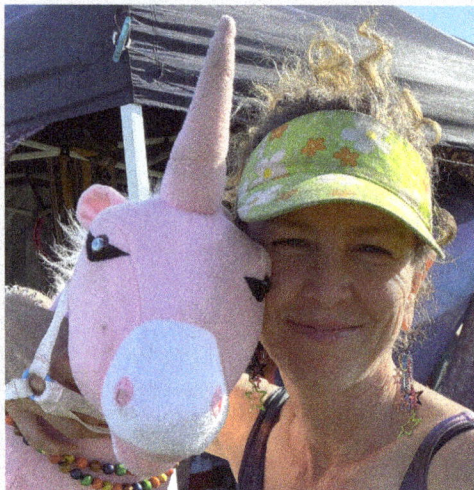

PREMA NISHAN - AUTHOR

The writer of this book knows very well the way of the wobble. She was a wild and woolly child, with a wobbly wallaby inside her, and, for whatever reasons, just couldn't behave as the adults told her to. Teachers and adults tried many strategies to 'discipline' her, including her grade five teacher regularly sending her to a small room in the office for hours on end – sometimes entire days - with nothing to do and nobody to talk to. It was there in that the little Prema discovered her inner bandicoot – that is, the mean character that dug it's home and stayed for quite awhile - that says that 'proper' people should be straight and not wobbly.

But the wallaby always knew better! Over the years, through a lot of work, she has learned to appreciate her inner wallaby – and has also made friends with her inner bandicoot! Just like in the story, the bandicoot has transformed into an ally – helping her to 'dig in straight lines' and follow systems when needed, and fit her creativity into the ways of the world. And the wallaby has taken her on many magical adventures, showed her much wonder and beauty in life. It is her hope that kids will grow up appreciating and loving their own inner creatures too!

Prema is trained as an art therapist, group facilitator and process-oriented counsellor. She has a master's degree in Conflict Management and Resolution, and her passion is helping people develop empathy and understand themselves and others more deeply, through process work and restorative justice practices. Her favourite things are dancing, growing food, cuddling her cat and making crazy cakes!

POLINA HRYTSKOVA - ILLUSTRATOR

I have loved drawing since early childhood. I grew up in a family of music teachers, without a father, in a small provincial town.

I graduated from college and worked as a teacher, designer, painted walls, painted icons, portraits, wrote poetry, sewed shoes in a factory, played keyboards in a rock band, was fond of woodcarving, sang in a church choir ...I like extreme entertainment: riding a motorcycle, parachuting, flying on a single-engine plane. I have performed in Ukraine, Poland and Russia with sand animation and I worked in Mexico, painting with sand (sand animation). I worked as a stage artist in America, in Hollywood, on the show "America's Got Talent" (backstage) and I created stage images, stage designs and decorations for different artists. I also collaborate with magicians, create drawings of illusion equipment, and design illusion devices (I once drew for David Copperfield!)

October 23rd 2020 I got married! I really want a lot of children, so far this is my greatest desire. I had a my first child- a beautiful baby girl - in June 2023. I continue to draw illustrations for children's books with more great pleasure. Now each of my illustrations is filled with fantastic tenderness and love, because I have a person with whom I share my imagination every day of my life!

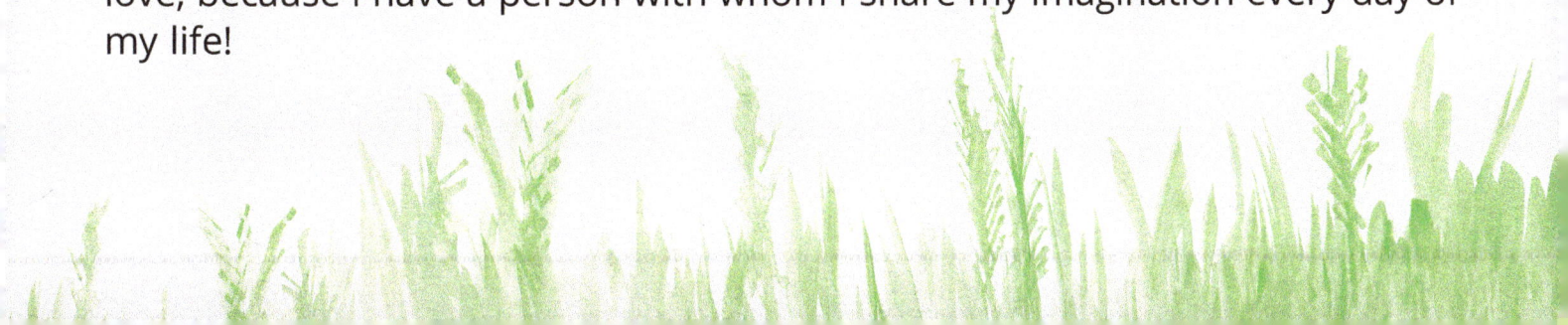

www.ingramcontent.com/pod-product-compliance
Lightning Source LLC
Chambersburg PA
CBHW060752150426

42811CB00058B/1389